Body Be Sound
poems

Georgia Tiffany

Encircle Publications, LLC
Farmington, Maine USA

Paperback ISBN-13: 978-1-64599-491-6

Editor: Cynthia Brackett-Vincent
Book and book cover design: Eddie Vincent/ENC Graphics Services
Cover Image: Marc Chagall
The Blue Circus (detail)
Oil on canvas, 349 × 267 mm
Collection of the TATE Museum (London, UK)
©2023 Artists Rights Society (ARS), New York / ADAGP, Paris
Author Photo: Amy Grey

Sign up for Encircle Publications newsletter and specials
http://eepurl.com/cs8taP

Mail Orders, Author Inquiries:
Encircle Publications
PO Box 187
Farmington, ME USA 04938
508-951-1996

Online orders:
encirclepub.com

In Memory of My Mother
Geraldine Bahr Cook Tiffany
(1915–2012)

for Ron
and for Mark, Michele, and Nicolle

TABLE OF CONTENTS

I

II

III

IV

I

BEFORE THE SNOW

From the pothole, tundra swans,
one, then the other, carry themselves
beyond the fence, beyond the horses,
glide into a winter light
that does not rise and will not fall.

November fog feathers the mesa
as if it were female, generously curved
and moist, granular sunsets
no longer chafing its entry
into the fractured coulee below.

In the scatter of sagebrush, pockmarked stone,
and grasses pressed into pools of slow wind
that tomorrow will freeze,
wild horses drink with their whole bodies,
then lift their heads into our gaze.

As one who has loved horses all her life,
my mother watches, her face flushed
with the love and the cold,
her legs dangling over the lowered tailgate.
"You should write a poem about this," she says,

brushing against my silent hand
her own, and I wonder
how long she has understood this country,
how long before she understands I never will.
"Seriously," she says.

Her hair, her lashes, too,
prematurely white, weightless as ash,
take on that mythic-blue tint of winter air
stirring in the way nerves stir
pretending to be reverent before sleep.

SOUTH DAKOTA SATURDAY NIGHT

My mother's younger sister in stocking feet, her shoes dangling
from one hand, the other hand easing open the screen door
and easing it closed, escapes into shadow. My mother lies on
the bed staring at a ceiling bright with starlight and longs
to risk the two-mile walk to Pickerel Lake. She imagines the
gathering community of Polish Catholic strangers she has been
warned to avoid. Polacks, her daddy calls them.

And though she's never dared be anything but the good girl,
she will not betray her sister's Saturday night escape across the
barren hills by moonlight to the forbidden barn where old men
unbutton their pressed shirts, lean against the moon-soaked
wood, smoke Lucky Strikes, tap their booted feet, and watch
the young, her sister among them, polka until the barn floor
will not stop throbbing.

Listening to cottonwoods and what she might have thought
she could hear, my mother must have pictured the boy who
escorted her sister back across the wheat fields, ducking under
one fence, over the next, kicking one leg, easing the other, until
they arrived at the border between land and desire, the grand
yielding fall of a full summer moon. She must have imagined
her own hand-sewn cotton dress frosted with starlight and the
sweet smell of being young, being a woman in love with the
one night of a South Dakota week belonging to bodies and
music.

MY MOTHER'S DANCE

Light must have begun with dancing.
Poised, breathless, she ventured
one foot out from under her long skirt,
then withdrew it
as if she'd touched fire.

It became a ritual—there in the kitchen—
a sacred opening of the blinds
and waiting for dawn.

Her body flushed with light,
she twirled in it, into it,
one-two-three, one-two-three,
bare feet across the linoleum
audible as breathing,
arms floating, hair unloosed.

And then the soft yes, *glissade*,
and yes again, a sudden Oh,
a pas de chat, *jeté, jeté.*

Did she see me there, behind the door,
half-awake and quivering,
my tightened calves presuming
a clumsy *relevé*
could lift me to such grace?

TOMATO PRESERVES

i.

Even if I had not been standing there,
close to her, with my whole body
open to morning, even if
I had still been asleep, burrowed and
dreaming under layers of cotton and wool,

I would have known—
lemon, cinnamon, ginger,
steaming through the open windows,
scenting the under-eaves,
as my mother, in her red headband,

eyes squinted against the heat,
tipped the heavy pan with both hands
and poured into each jar
the hot syrup, bright with
translucent strips of lemon peel

floating over the lip, the tomatoes
tightly packed, radiant as they trembled
just enough to make room,
the slow syrup fondling its way
down and through the gaps between.

ii.

Come late September, year after year,
it had been my job
to carry the still-warm jars,
step by step, one by one,
down the stairs.

In the closet-sized room
steeped in earthy underground odors,
used fruit boxes and weathered boards
lined the length of each wall
from ceiling to floor.

Between these makeshift shelves
and with hardly space to turn around,
I teetered on the old milking stool
and pulled the chain.
Instant streams of orange and honey,

lavish vermilion and gold,
rippled the dizzied room,
bulb swinging, jars shrugging off
their accustomed dark,
tomatoes exposed and luminous.

My breath disturbs nothing now—
not the spider in the corner,
not the long-abandoned shelves.
"The pantry," my mother called it.
My father called it, "Your mother's room."

BLESSING

We waited for his head to lift from grace,
his hand to take up the linen napkin,
shake it loose from its fold,
drape it over one leg.
It was the sign.

I took up my own, fingering the initial T
stitched in the corner,
and smoothed it across my lap.
My crinoline petticoat rustled.
We waited for his hand to lift the spoon,

then the intrusive clink
of silver on china,
my sister's glass of milk
pressed to her lip and the nervous sip,
mostly my own internal swallowing.

Her chair scraping against the floor,
Mother pushed back from the table.
"Should I turn on the Mozart?"
I stopped chewing,
looked first toward my mother's question,

then to my father's jaw,
and buried my gaze in the platter of carrots,
potatoes, chunks of beef.
Breath waited inside me so deep, so long
I could hear its echo.

At last, "Yes," muttered my father.
Mother's Sunday shoes
pattered across the kitchen floor
and entered the plush pile of the living room.
There was a fumbling,

a click, a pause,
and the 78 dropped to the turntable.
We heard the arm rise,
adjust itself, land the needle
with a tiny scratch to find the groove.

The mass began. "Mozart," my mother said
to no one in particular, scooting her chair
back under the table,
her voice a whisper that had too far to go.
"The Kyrie. I love the Kyrie."

OUR DAILY BREAD

Floured with light, my mother concentrates
as though she's never made bread before,
as though her hands have just now
discovered how flour
accumulates in the creases,

embeds itself under her nails.
She leans her weight into her hands,
presses them into the dough
and folds the dough into a ball.
Her hands pause, and her voice

floats toward the open window
like a quiet vapor that contains the world.
We dream toward loneliness, she says
as if it were the whole story.
I saw a coyote chew off her own paw.

Rotating the dough, she kneads again,
autumn swelling up and down another dawn
of dry earth and South Dakota wind.
I listen as if I already understand
wind can break us in two.

She cradles the loaf, eases it into the pan.
*Your great grandmother had one eye
larger than the other.
She saw her father kill a buffalo.
She slept with him under the hide.*

Almost thirteen, I don't know how I know,
but I know all our lives she will do this,
gaze out the kitchen window
beyond bitterbrush and little hives of dust
toward the fallow field

where starlings feed under some shape
a cloud is trying to remember.
Quickened by my new breasts,
I tighten my fists
because what my mother says—it might be true.

DISGRACE

"Why me?" I asked, all the way to the dark,
where I'd practiced my whole life,
where I'd shamed my father.
"Beethoven," I'd told him, "was a pure romantic."
"No!" he said. "Passion is technique,
a way to control."

Sitting in the first row, he had prepared to hear.
But I played the *Appassionata*
and something came into my fingers
that was not my fingers,
that was not the long hours of arpeggios, scales,

all those hours my mother sat on the couch
knitting, insisting
on arpeggios and scales,
all those Saturday nights my father,
in his burgundy chair after supper,
commanded, "Play what you've learned."

I was accumulating, but I did not know
and my father did not know.
"Faster, cleaner," he said.
"Next week, sevens, seven to a beat."
I was heading for a past that had conceived me,
what I did not know.

And there, in the first row, sat my father,
stunned by passion, not believing his own blood
had driven the music this far out of control.
"You've disgraced me," he said,
"disgraced us both."
Mother made a conjugal gesture.

The adjudicator said, "Never
have I heard in one so young,"
he lifted his eyebrows, "such passion."
In that thrall, the mind must let go or else
remember what it does not know.
That's how it happened.

"It was not music," my father announced,
frowning down the whole length of the breakfast table.
"Beethoven was deaf," I did not say.

MILKMAN

Frosted with their own cold,
bottles clink in his wire carrier.
To the milkman's amazement,
my mother opens the door
in her chiffon peignoir,
poses, one hand on the doorknob,
one bare foot resting on the other,
body shivering.

Snow hardly beginning yet,
and yet certain as the gutters
slow glistening with hoarfrost,
she bends to take up the bottles,
a thin layer of cream
visible in the neck of each,
and lifts her eyes to the body of him
stark against the dawn
making his way back down the walk.

The light behind her, the shape of her
inside the gown, translucent skin of her,
unbrushed hair curling to her shoulders,
my fledgling self
hugging my fledgling self
flannel-clad and aching to be that beautiful,

I'll stir autumn after autumn
into the warm milk of her,
her naked feet, her half-open mouth,
the way she pressed a cold bottle to her lips
as if to taste the entire world
and thought to follow him,
milk truck sliding down our icy street.

THE LAST THEOREM

i.

My father believed mathematics
the key to the world,

my father being the one who chose
to slip out of the equation
one plus one equals three.

I think of this now as I pass the place
where the apple tree grew,

and how before language
he would lay two apples in my lap,
mime one plus one equals . . .

then point to me, repeating the act
and adding the words until I believed,

and how, after language,
he quoted Bertrand Russell loosely
as a reply to my mother's need:

"I like mathematics; it does not
require us to love it back."

ii.

Studying Greek mathematics late into the night,
Pierre de Fermat scribbled, "There's no solution,"
in the margin of *Arithmetica*, a margin so narrow,
he did not have space to write the proof.

Because an elliptical curve that could not exist
fit an equation that should not exist,
Andrew Wiles, in 1993, proved the unproven,
for three centuries only imagined.

Scholars crossed themselves and kneeled.
Who would not want to feel the holiness
of all that human time devoted
to the margin of an ancient book?

What part of me is lost if I cannot?
And yet, I am in awe of the secluded Wiles,
haunted since childhood by an elusive proof,
and I wonder if anyone ever kissed him

so close to the brain the signals got confused?
Perhaps his mother, counting his fingers and toes,
rejoiced that he would be perfect
if only he could love her more.

iii.

Every night, my mother counted stitches
and listened to Brahms.
The afghan grew to cover her lap, her feet,

spilled onto the floor,
and flowed out the door, across the lawn,

into the field beside the house,
through the crackle of wheat, and beyond
the wheat, a geometry of stars.

She found pleasure in this, as a soul
finds pleasure in counting, said Leibniz,

without being aware.
Music, my mother said, pleased
with the thought of not being aware.

The house is gone, the apple tree gone.
I can still hear the click of the needles

cast off, cast on
and Brahms' elusive twos against threes,
the way they disturb the air.

I would count roots, stars,
morality simplified to Fibonacci numbers:

the future without the present
is the past; the present without the past
cannot survive.

But Dear Mathematics,
do you require too much or too little?

Does the danger lie in the mind or the body?
Divide the child by a knife—what's
the answer to that?

Will worlds, once again, fall to their knees
and repeat, "There is no solution"?

VOW

He was driving me away, and away
I would forget
the dashboard lit like a carnival,
my father's foot pumping the gas,
his touch on my thigh.

He was taking me to the university,
Wagner too loud on the radio,
a fat left hand too full of fingers
gripping the wheel.
I stared across pale hills.

My fingers on the safety glass,
nothing else seemed real—
not the two-bedroom house, the tall poplar,
laundry dripping from the line;
not the woman fighting the wind.

I shall never be ordinary, I vowed
to the woman, to the laundry,
to my mother in the rearview mirror.
I bleached and bleached it all away,
and hung from the line,

to hang being a verb for cleanliness,
a synonym for some brightly white being
clothespinned and flailing.
or else, perhaps,
a lie in love with wind.

WHISPERS

i.

We begin on the other side of dark
and afterwards invent a reason.
That's what my mother told me,

rocking under the porch light,
sipping from a Haviland cup
and petting the Angora,

fingers deep in the long hair
or else toying with her own.
I was whispering to confess.

She said she had loved often,
and understood. The moths, she said,
how confused they seem,

who think they could be stars,
but they are sorrow.
All sundown she had been watching.

It was the spaniel I watched,
digging under mother's begonias,
his jaw full of bone.

ii.

Blame it on morning fog, black ice,
brakes that gripped too suddenly;
blame my mother.

Her Olds flew from the bridge,
hit the pine and folded,
scraped off branches all the way down.

The femur snapped, the leg dangled,
and someone moaned,
who could have been me, or else

my mother, her hands slipping off the wheel.
Someone says, "That door, that one."
Mother says she can still hear

the assembly of strangers
breathing over my life,
still see the surgeon, his hands full of limb.

The moths have followed us here.
Like the dead, they are everywhere.
They inhale. They inhale.

iii.

The leg hangs above me,
for seven weeks my only love.
My mother thinks I need hers.

She brushes my hair, arranges
and rearranges the sheets, the room,
turns the air on and off,

revisits my sleep.
Who are you? I would ask,
but it takes too much breath.

She could be the death-shift;
she could be the moon
that crashed five feet from White River

wrong side up, and yet,
the delicate mouth on the lip of the cup,
the translucent eye that will not shut,

the Madame Alexander doll
with porcelain leg and heart,
missing patent leather shoe . . .

iv.

My mother writes this.
She has assumed my voice
as if I'm in her head.

Her pen scratches at the dark
a hole to crawl through
searching for lines worth returning for.

It's stoic, the tubers she winters over
knuckled and dry in the cellar,
the begonias she insists on planting every year.

Heirloom scarlet, they flower soft-mouthed,
bent-pitched, fragile to the touch
and bruised like an old injury,

every bruise my mother's apology
as if she were responsible.
How can I tell her

dark begins on both sides?
The moths could be in my head.
Like good bone, she writes, I could mend.

STROKE

My mother calls leaves feathers,
the poem in her head flying
between memory and one final autumn—
a rupture of blight and gold.
She says the feathers cry out like humans
when their mouths go dry.

Cowled in shadow, my mother
sits at our old Baldwin
pumping her bare foot
against the sustaining pedal.
She has opened the music and
confronts the notes as if
she could blame Rachmaninoff.
She says chickadees
are dancing across her eyes.

On the night before her dead baby,
I lay in my mother's arms
and touched her swollen belly.
The baby will love you, my mother said,
as much as I do.
She remembers this now.

SUNDAY DRIVE

When my mother asks, "Why
can't we take a nice Sunday drive
like we used to?" I do not think
about history, not how we reinvent it,
or why, for I am consumed with wishing

someone else would bundle her up,
someone else help her
shuffle down the sidewalk to the car
in this early October chill,
someone else relive the history—

stores closed on the Sabbath,
my sister and I piled into the back seat
fighting over comic books,
Betty and Veronica, Superman,
my father at the wheel

thumping his index finger
and counting to five for silence,
my mother cowering next to him,
wearing that silly pillbox hat
she always wore on Sunday.

"Don't you remember cowering?"
I want to remind her, his old white Ford
bumping east toward Montana
or north into Spirit Lake country, or south,
stubbled wheatfields, the day

a firmament of hawks and slow passage
under their developed eye,
my father explaining geology,
my mother listening
to insects feasting on dry peas,

my sister eventually asleep,
while I pick at a scab on my knee,
both of us dreaming of another history,
one that will not consume
the rest of our lives.

"Is it Sunday?" my mother wants to know,
hatless now, me driving
a familiar dirt road toward the river,
chattering about heron we would watch
if there were heron, if we could see.

She slumps against the seatbelt.
Her fingers stroke the wool afghan
I've draped over her lap
and tucked under her legs,
all that is gone by October gone—

mating rites, migrating birds, tourists
in their white shorts and canoes.
By tomorrow, winter will have closed the road.
She is sure of it.
"Is it still Sunday?" she asks again.

ABSENCE

i.

Just one lonely county after another.
Here, and there,
a carnal mark of distance—
collapsed roof,
flailing barbed wire in the wind,

my mother (seventeen years old,
bare feet planted tentatively,
tendril of hair,
crescent moon of its shadow
cut across her forehead)

stares across a country
burned up in the sun,
diverging roads,
a decision that could mean something,
could mean nothing.

ii.

We're heading back with the ashes.
Is anything less real
than anything else?
This car full of summer heat,
this urn of secrets, this part of her

that is landscape,
the landscape that is my mother.
Can anyone ever look at this country
without a deluge of locusts,
or a stray at the screen door,

or the way wind
folds loss under the eave,
scours out the house,
leaves its moans
in the bedroom hollows?

iii.

The night my father did not come home
my mother said you could love
something like that to death.
She meant the absence.
But what to do with the stray?

Seeing it there at the screen door,
is it possible
from the first lifted paw,
the muted whine,
she knew about the other dogs,

and the girl who would love them,
lie with them
bundled in animal sleep
or spread-eagle in the safe refuge
of an abandoned corn row?

HOMETOWN BURIAL

i.

Morning glares across fields
pungent and newly drowned.
The ball diamond wallows in mud.

Along the state road into town
a barn trapped in receding waters
tilts, oddly proud

as if the walls had always slanted,
the roof had always gaped with holes.
We've driven inland a thousand miles.

At the Red Horse Inn
they tell us a wet spring
overwhelmed the ditches,

flooded the highway,
and roadside ponds are offering up fish
to anyone who works a rod.

A mounted walleye in the lounge
(the sign says nineteen pounds)
hangs above the couch.

ii.

It's late June, a month of insects
hackberry leaves bladed with sunlight,
my mother's gravesite wet

but resistant. Two men take turns
plunging the auger,
easy in their seasoned hands,

the home-fired urn awkward in mine.
Not until we arrived in South Dakota,
not until we stood at the gravesite

would I dare to think,
"This is not my mother.
My mother is not here."

But here she is. This ash of a body.
And if I could put it back together,
would she know it for the first time?

I take the photo next to her marker:
two men she never knew, my sister,
and in the distance, swamps of summer corn.

THE VISIT

My mother knocks at the door.
She carries a pale blue bowl
on which a hand-painted woman
has gathered her skirts to her hips
and wades in the river.

My mother knows I am home.
She has seen a light in the window
and wonders why I closed the curtains
which are also pale blue.
Her voice cannot get through.

I would answer the door,
but she is sorrow,
and a hole the size of the moon
has opened behind her.
Nothing about her seems familiar,

not her face, marbled with shadow,
not the way her eyes widen as if a terror
had seized her from the inside out,
a thick night of sycamores
closing around her.

There's a quiver in her strangeness,
one hand still balancing the bowl, the other
too heavy, like a stone.
She knocks again.
There is only the bowl.

II

PORTRAIT

Small globs of paint have hardened,
the image hardened, too,
dry to the touch. And yet,
the flesh appears wet. The lips. The cheeks.
It's a technique to lose the heart in.

With gaze not exactly captured,
more like unfinished,
misformed eyebrows unfinished too,
renegade tuft of hair, skin
a grief of light about the bones,

how unimportant it seemed
in the dark corner of the gallery.
How unattended.
How abandoned the air around it.
Still, you could not turn away.

What strange power compelled you
as though you had no choice?
Not then. Not now.
The child's head tilts, the painting tilts—
this portrait you purchased, took home

thinking to love it out of sadness,
hung it over the dresser like a mirror.
Three a.m. Too late to shake loose
this ruin of sleep, too early to rise,
moonlight through the dormer window

shrinking and swelling as if it could breathe,
as if it could teach the child to breathe,
as if lunar breath might
change everything—
what you see, what you cannot see.

NIGHTWALK

You can hear them
through the open windows,
voices you recognize
making little sounds
you recognize,
performing little acts
you know of,
doing it all in the dark
and you shuffling through
the last of an October rain,
hardly a rain at all, mostly
locust leaves' half-hearted
letting go, mostly,
your arms tight around your body,
hips moving like a secret,
silk nightie cold and
clinging beneath your coat,
the sudden need for breathing in
this raw chill of moon
only just now stalking your shadow.

THIS IS NOT A POEM ABOUT BIRDS

i.

First they honk, one, then another,
an almost symmetrical V,
four on one side, five on the other,

trailing the point bird through heat,
their cries abrasive with smoke,
the distance around us burned and burning.

My neighbor's tabby glances up.
Perhaps he'd think to fly,
but he is eighty-some in human years,

content to merely roam beneath the yews
where neighborhood quail
teach their chicks to fear.

This year September is symmetrical—
fire, no fire, fire again, a kind of triptych
like love or war—

my disposable mask symmetrical too,
with adjustable noseclip,
collapse resistant,

electrostatically charged microfiber
designed to ease the breathing.

ii.

Through Saturday morning market
we wander—to say "like ghosts"
would be too easy.

The few who have come wear masks,
people I know or do not know, vendors,
even small children, masked.

Not the thick ocher air,
block after block of abandoned stalls,
unsold peaches, apricots, turnip greens,

not the scorched hills above town,
clusters of elderberries heaped
with ash, blue-black, blue-black,

not drifts of stubble gone gray,
or the maples turned alarmingly red,
or the paralyzing fatigue,

not the fires spreading north and south,
east and west, thirteen percent contained,
but the children, singing,

and the geese leaving us
to sort it out for ourselves.

SUMMONED

All the bones of the ear are tested here,
the river so quiet I can hear
spiders weaving their lives together,
fish kissing the stones,
nests unraveling to let last sunlight through.

Surely others have come this way,
and yet the path along the shore
seems hardly worn,
mostly a wandering of autumn grasses
menacing my calves,

an occasional dizzy call tumbling
from high above language or snow,
and one blue heron stiffly poised, untended
except as sudden gusts
crosshatch the backwater with light.

Could this be his moment,
the way light swirls down and around
and through him, or is it
just a flush of being
that turns him suddenly ablaze,

my mortal pose paralyzed,
fetal and braced against the dusk,
the shallows limpid,
a summoned breath withholding,
withheld?

Do I hear the feathers tremble
before the wings
(so labored they seem resistant)
lift the body skyward
trailing their six-foot span of shadow?

Is there a presence of mind, a guardian
that tends so holy its watch?
I can see it, if I see anything at all,
only as motion
bearing the river away.

ON THE SUBJECT OF GHOSTS

i.

My aunt devotes herself to riding horses,
says motion must surely please the universe,
says that's the only way to feel the soul.

Later, she sketches how the muscles
still move beneath her, pencils lines
in rapid repetition to depict the run.

At one time, she tells me, a running horse
can have all four feet off the ground.
Just think on it.

Brush in hand, she gazes at the canvas,
begins a rhythmic sway, side to side,
envisions the place motion might appear,

then dips and glides the paint into the mane.
Madly more paint. More mane. More wind.
Still a mystery, the body waits,

but my aunt has put her brush down.
It's no use, she says.
I'm painting shadows.

ii.

Of the skull of a horse buried
under the hearthstone, of the one
in the floor, and the one in the wall,

of equine skulls kingdoms old
under bridges, church altars,
my aunt says we can hear

what moves inside all
these resonant chambers, these
intricate pathways, cavities

of secrets, omens, gods overheard,
underheard, she says,
these fine hearty echoes.

Through these bones, the blood,
the nerves to the brain.
Through these thirty-four bones

centuries of heartbeat.
Press your ear right here.
Feet dancing. Pillow talk. Human song.

iii.

I think of horses now—their skulls filled with echoes
and that touch of earth, that surge
of bodies they are surely dreaming back to.

I imagine them flowing through ponderosas
or along the river under wing
of some great bird, or asleep in the center

of folding and unfolding clouds.
A poet writes, "They wait until the wind comes
and gallop in their stillness again."

If I press my hand to that stillness,
will I feel the breath, the heartbeat?
My aunt says horses hear ghosts.

Brush in hand, she's at it again,
swaying side to side, listening for the place
where ghosts might appear.

Her need to complete nothing
fills the spare room with unfinished canvases
she's planning to save for another life.

IN THE DRY SEASON

Rumors of rain sink deep and deeper,
seep underground,
caress dead roots as if they still matter.

Tracks the harvester left years ago
gouge the hills where
heat waves over hard-baked clay

shimmer without apology.
Everywhere eyes still nervous.
Everywhere the phantom sway of wheat.

You're driving along the old riverbed
that divides field from played-out field,
pasture from overgrazed pasture—

miles of barbed wire,
cedar posts no longer sound
casting shadows like curses.

Reckless, the way you take the curves,
sometimes pulling too much to the right,
sometimes to the left,

an occasional wheel in the gravel shoulder
spitting stones at the undercarriage,
dead bee on the windshield.

The ache for the land is in the air around you,
in the way you roll down the window,
taste the failure.

Who can blame you for praising
the one beautiful thing—
cinnamon-red tail feathers,

four-foot wingspan, white underbelly
riding the thermal updraft high and higher—
this one beautiful thing

that waits only on itself
hovering in anticipation?
What does it care of you,

who wait, too, for the spectacular
swoop to violence,
legs extended, talons stretched,

the sweet divinity of the strike,
you, whoever you are now,
wanting to invent excuses

for the sake of beauty,
wanting to be closer,
a rush in the groin wanting to be the kill?

IN THE NIGHT THE RAIN BEGINS
for RBG

The smell of sleep around me
and the sun burning out,
basalt grates against the sky,
September absorbing its grief
and that reluctant loss of heat.

Tundra swans out of the coulee,
wide wings surprised by
how heavy evening rides,
attempt to inhabit a gesture upward,
falter, and fail,
eyes glazed with their turn from
light we once embraced
as what this land has loved and bled for.

I'm calling out, calling
so hard my throat catches
raw with sage,
and rain, the first in months, begins
as if I'd summoned it
by some extraordinary will,
the air above me flooding
with the sound of rain.

Lost as any country now,
as far as I can see
mourned by these stumbling words.
Winter waiting.

BEAR ON THE ROAD TO THE SUN

Early October, still warm in the body,
she'd stopped to stretch her legs
and let the engine cool,

the river, the highway,
the sharp whistle of osprey,
all below her calling her down.

Just an impulsive college girl
eager for the mile-high view, she
had ignored predictions, an ominous sky

scraping against her old Valiant
as it climbed toward the pass.
Height seemed not so high

as sacred, a lightheadedness
she was not prepared for, and suddenly
the knowledge she had come too far.

Grey hair on the lifted muzzle
and under the throat,
the grizzly seemed content

to loom and sway,
to flex his great jaw, swell his girth,
slowly rear as if he ruled the continent.

She thought to be afraid,
and yet, for no reason she could explain,
she needed him to take possession,

to offer some sign
that he beheld beyond appetite
her being there.

The mountain released a vapor,
the bear retreating into it,
into the great white ghost of it,

and believing she had the power
to return the way she came,
she pushed on after him,

each step weighing more than the last,
each pause aware
that the next step would sink deeper,

that something inside the mountain
would crack, and sound rise from the belly
as from the glacial prowl of him.

Impossible to separate bear
from mountain, mountain from
thickening snowfall,

flesh from the curse of it,
still she pursued as though she could see,
hauling her body toward the Divide

while around her closed
the intimate dark of bear odor
and her intoxicating own.

How does one explain the beloved?
At what point did she know?
Would it be in the news?

One more girl in love with the mountain
lured from the road
and mauled for virgin blood.

ROADKILL

If not for the lump of fur
would I have noticed
the blood-stained gravel at the roadside—
only a few stones, really—dry now
but carmine in the pre-dusk light?

How long did I squat by the body
wondering what tore the head off,
launched it twenty feet away
into thistle where it lodges still?
Is there a consciousness on duty,

not beauty, but beautiful nonetheless,
as if the two had not been severed
and the same power
that kept the body dancing
could keep the head alive?

Did the claws lash out
before the muscles seized,
the nerves recoil, the marrow stall?
Would the coyote wait,
the buzzards pause to feed?

That violence had been done is certain.
The air aches with the smell of it,
a sudden shadow
evidence even stillness fails.
Possum? The neighbor's cat?

Too dark to tell.
I can't see my hand, can't see
my fingertips, or knuckles,
or whether the veins, blue as lobelia,
still pump with the work of dying.

IF LIGHT COULD HOWL

At first I thought something other than myself
spooked the trees.
A snake, two feet long and pausing
as if to wait me out,
slid from the trail into the brush
and then paused again
the sleek, striped ending of him there
to be admired.

I had returned to the river
somewhere between the heron feeding
and the heron gone.
I thought I had come alone.
Instead, the daylight fleeing,
the snake waiting,
and this other shadow that stops when I stop
and takes hold of my arm.

When I open my mouth, it is alive with bees;
when I close it, they crawl into the brain
like so many dying things
and feast there.
This could be a dream,
but my eyes are swollen as if they've been stung
and the inner circle of the sun
turns black with pollen.

TROUBLE WITH HOLY PLACES

The first time he held a rifle
he thought it weighed more than God

and hauled it into a draw
where tracks crossed and recrossed

an excess of moonlight high as his thighs
and stained with blood.

He did not hear—never heard—
the silence quicken, circle back, reclaim

what might have been holy.
He would not have recognized it if he had.

Who said a hunter must love what he hunts,
and honor whatever he kills?

For he loved nothing then, not honor,
not the pelt stripped from the body,

not the body or the brain or the crosshairs
or the complicit scope.

Years later, he discovered tracks again
long under snow, and followed

as one might follow words
one cannot think to say

across a field scarred by language
and giving no hint of what might

or might not next arrive.
Is that when everything turned metaphor,

as if metaphor itself were holy?
It was not a question he knew to ask.

But suddenly the night stirred as the loins
stir as the beast stirs for its own,

and he found himself inside himself
with a coyote for a heart.

THE PHOTO I KEPT

*The magpie, omnivore of the Channeled Scablands, often
chooses to feast on the dead. Stunningly beautiful, and
very intelligent, it is one of the few animal species that can
recognize itself in a mirror.*

i.

Every winter he hunted the scabs.
He knew how pelts thicken
and breath can freeze at forty below,

how soon the moon reshapes
tracks of coyotes,
how fast the wind can carry them away.

He needed the three-sixty view,
those miles and miles to anywhere
that preserve illusion

and how a whiteout can remove
all distinctions
that get in the way.

In spring, he loved the snakes
he learned to tame, storms at Banks
that flushed the rattlers out,

the lakeshore choked with them,
his small boat trapped for days,
and how at night a storm could end

so suddenly the explosion of stars
would blind him,
the quiet too quiet, like serpents mating,
or else waiting in his throat for time.

ii.

On weekends, Jake's father bet the dogs,
sent him to Wallace or Kellogg
to pick up a few bucks, maybe a girl.

Everyone said it. Dean Martin's voice.
"Welcome to my World," he'd croon
or thump out "Leroy Brown" and take a hit or two.

At fourteen, in the parking lot of a Butte saloon,
he was raped by two whores
with, he said, "nothing better to do."

As insects know the enemy's not wind
though wind is cruel, he knew the drill.
Compose. Decompose.

He dealt blackjack, ran the pawn shop,
beat a coke addiction,
saved an undercover cop from extinction

and won the year's "Outstanding Citizen,"
had his son christened Methodist
so he would not be Jew.

A trooper found the son in white robes
wandering coyote country barefoot
and calling, "Father, Father,"
the nightsnow armed with stars.

iii.

I don't know who took the photo.
Jake standing on Steamboat Rock,
a dead rattler draped around his neck,

poses against the sun, feet apart,
hands, too large for the body,
hanging at his sides

and trembling in a wind of heat,
hands that could pound out "Piano Man"
with a fifth of vodka, and a chaser

of any woman so buried in shadow
only the dead could take him
deep enough down.

Once a flood ravaged this entire basin,
gouged out canyons 200 feet down,
carried car-sized boulders 500 miles.

Now buttes rise like ragged altars
that have outlived the water.
From every direction, the marmots return.

Upright on their haunches,
they shake their little fists at the sun.
Yet still I hear Jake shouting,
"In this land, not even the ghosts survive."

NIGHT FISHING

Is a man thinking in the night, the night?
  —Li-Young Lee

A tug on the line
is only her shadow come down.
She lays the pole on the dock and
dips a hand in water,
interrupts her face and the dark begins.
The moon begins in her hand, tiny
moon hairs crawl her fingers, her forearm.

In the swamp, frog of a thousand voices.
In the water, moon of a thousand lures.
In the moon, man of a thousand
passions in the body
of a girl so quiet the fish
do not neglect her, do not neglect her
astonishing.

Wind leafs its way through secret water,
though the aspen are not
visible in the dark, though the dark
is not visible,
and leaves and secrets which are not
secrets exactly,
but a collection of nerves,
tangle in motion.
An old fisherman lifts his from the sea.

MANATEE

If she sang, I could not hear her,
nor did I see the huge hump of body
submerged and feeding in the cove,
hundreds of pounds
moving unlike the mythic mermaid
of her fabled ancestry
but more like art
creating the need for itself.

For this grand seacow of a body
to be beautiful—
this ancient, too gentle, grazer of the sea,
mouth full of turtle grass,
water hyacinth and mangrove leaves,
this opulent bulk
of wrinkled skin and whiskered snout
surfacing to breathe
and breathing to remember
the world she thought she knew—

for this grand seacow to be beautiful
had nothing to do with the world
and everything to do
with her solitary swimming upside down,
her identifying scars,
and the way she rolled darkly
feminized by the sea.

LOW TIDE

Seaglow around you. Hum of wings.
Quiet of sound among secrets.
You can hear the sea sucking, hear
creatures open and close
folded in creases of the sea.

But the ruins are what you listen for,
ancient hulls on the seabed,
ghosts watery and awash
in the muscle memory of some other life.

If you could be that other life,
an inexhaustible being of erotic
burials and resurrections,
you might ask, "Where is the body?"

Saltwater churns up from the ruins
in white pools, goes down in spume,
gulls circling, a starfish on bright sand,
bleached bones resurfacing.

If you held the bones in your hand
could you hear them?
What would you do with such joy?
Would you hush it, strum it?
Would you call out its name? . . .
Joy. Oh, archetypal Joy.

You can see it from the shore
in the heave and spend of waves so far away
they must be imagined
and yet, that wide stretch into distance
warms the dead around you.

Why do you hesitate?
Just look how far the body has carried you
suspended, magenta,
sweet smelling as beach peas
all the way across water where wind plays
translucent as a mermaid's spine.
How long will you wait to decide?

TROUBLE WITH MINNOWS

They arrived by starlight
filling up the dark
and barking their tiny breaths.
I should have turned on the stereo,
listened to Mozart, or pieced together
the puzzle of a little Austrian village
that restored itself after the war—
painted its shutters, its window boxes,
planted geraniums.

But tonight, it's minnows.
They slam against the window,
swim back and forth across
the violence they do.
How small their bones must be!
Or do they have bones at all,
do they exist purely by motion and move
merely to move?

More bearable than angels,
they do not speak of revolution,
they do not speak of love.
They trust the current,
hunger themselves against each other,
thicken their lips for kisses.
They think they are harmless.

It's three in the morning.
Someone somewhere is preparing to wake,
someone to sigh, someone to weep.
I simply want to sleep, or rather
to sleep simply.
Instead, I am measuring myself
against the end of things,

how a puzzle breaks apart too easily,
how the minnows stir up
a sadness they cannot swim through.

Long into dawn, I'll drift on the minnows'
mindless impulse to increase
their kind of feeding in the world,
and I confess an envy
for their guiltless intimacies,
their reckless grace.

III

VENUS OF HOHLE FELS

i.

To carve from a mammoth's tusk
the fingers of her,
the seams of her,
the fecund fullness of her,
archaeologists guessed hundreds of hours,
called her fertility goddess,
essence of female,

this Venus
six centimeters tall
hung as an amulet around the neck,
or enshrined on a ceremonial wall.

Mycelium draped her breasts,
garlands of roots over her, under her,
worms fondling
the rough-hewn cleavages of her,
thirty-five thousand years
seeped into fissures
where time made room for dawn.

ii.

Some thought she'd come off the mountain
to wander the valley,
to drink from the Aach
or bathe in the Blau.

Some said she'd blessed
the souls of the dying
or knelt at the feet of their gods.

Others supposed she'd been a mate,
or maybe a neighbor who posed,
unwrapped herself
that season she became woman
in the palm of a hand.

Six fragments of her unearthed
ten feet underground,
the pieces glued together—
the bounty of her
still missing an arm, a shoulder, a head.

iii.

Who would be her priest?
For she already imagined
breathing not for mere breath
in small, sputtering gulps
but as one breathes with a grand inhaling
pleasure of new air,
rose all petal and pollinating bees,
queen (before diadem and scepter)
of gardens already imagined
(when small birds sighed,
she would sigh),
coupling with Mars,
daughter of Jove, mother of Cupid,
protectress of Caesar and myrtle-crowned,
all already imagined
before rising from the foam of the sea,
before before.

iv.

She had looked down at what, by touch,
she found to be her own body

and saw (already imagined)
the exuberant breasts,
lifted one, then the other,
felt the ribs beneath,
encountered the fine swell of belly,
opulent thighs,
labial flower floating,

and took up the tool
to scrape from the ivory tusk
what was not breast,
what was not thigh,
what was not pelvis, arms, hands,
and so on about the body,
and she would know herself
by what she left
and what she scraped away.

v.

They move like mourners.
(they would see, they would not see)
Museum lights expose each fold,
each undulant fall of flesh,
striated pelvis,
buttocks generous.

(they would touch, they cannot touch)
Morning star. Evening star.
(a litany of whispers)
Appalling. Pornographic.
Grotesque.
(they would move on

to knives and spearheads,
hand axes and awls)

Such a fuss
over something so small.
(they cannot move on)
She's the new star of Blaubeuren now.

vi.

And what of you, sitting here,
weary with seeking words already fled
before you can think them,
pen limp in your hand,
watching a goldfinch
drink from her reflection in the copper bath?

Why do you persist to burrow
in layers of dark where you have already
spent too many nights
not in soothing moonlight, but in musky toxins
and perfumes of this Venus
you would deify?

You have heard her in her songs as you slept,
owl by night, cave swift by echo,
monarch in the milkweed
flinging into distant worlds the way wind moves
and does not move,
survival in every little thing.

There was a woman told
she could never see the light
unless she lived in darkness.
She took to her bed
the tusk of ivory,
slept through the winter

with it pressed to her body
as a mystery to be suddenly revealed
and rose to all she'd imagined.
She would have you bathe her with sweet oils,
wrap her in soft linen.
She would have you finish the story.

DAGUERREOTYPE OF UNIDENTIFIED WOMAN

(Mathew Brady, c.1861)

She grows accustomed to the sound of taffeta,
the way he takes the fabric
between his index finger and thumb,
rubs it like a thought he had
and would have again.

She grows accustomed to the bonnet bow
too snug around her neck,
the cascade of ringlets—are they hers,
or just a dream she dreamed
to be undone?

Her mouth inclined like an experiment,
her lips sensitized with iodine
and exposed, her gaze all but vanished,
yet fixed in vapor, she stares
as if she were real enough to die.

What she sees she does not see.
What he sees, like light in a darkroom,
cannot be trusted.
Surely she knew.
Still, he speaks in ever afters,

he who left his fingerprint on her collar,
all lace and delicate as her white hands
irreverently ungloved,
he who astonished the moment
to own it.

BETWEEN A MAN AND A WOMAN

They're driving west through quiet that oppresses,
visor low, wires of light spidering out the sun.
They do not speak.
They have not spoken for miles.

Between her vision and the afternoon heat,
the horses come,
ears backfolded, bellies tight,
and balance at the edge of sky, their silhouettes
astride this silence she could call home
if only he would touch her now,
break into breathing
like so many horses rising out of the sea.

But the man does not see the horses.
He has focused on the yellow line,
held the speedometer at sixty,
planted his hands on the wheel at ten and two.

They pant like gods, the woman says.
Their blue backs shine, their hooves shine.
They seduce their own bones.

How slowly she feels her way out of body,
how easily rides wave after wave
over creature ruins, over beaked outcroppings
and fossil poplars sinking
into all they have flowered of shadow.

And when she turns so utterly breathable,
no other air could inhabit his blood so well.

He would open his lungs, say yes,
yes to the rhythm of horses,

yes to himself possessed
if only the road would stop rocking
and the distance dissolve.

Dusk coppers the gorge, powders the flanks
of sumac descending the draw.
And then she's dusk on the tongue,
light that flows free from his last glimpse of her
in the rearview mirror,
night wind consuming a sky without horses.

WHAT MY GRANDMOTHER SAID

There is no love apart from the deeds of love;
—Jean-Paul Sartre

Maybe because my grandfather left her
not much more than a girl
with three children, locusts, the farm,
and everything shy about her
a kind of turbulence,
she preferred the cellar,

or maybe the furnace soothed her,
the quiet underground—
cobwebs stirring as the air stirred,
floor joists creaking with footsteps above her,
and always the possibility
of coming up from the going down.

The mending room she called it,
chose that space in the basement where
each morning I could find her,
cast iron treadle under her pumping foot,
cast iron trademark in capitals
two inches high: SINGER.

And she did sing, content
among the sounds of belt and band wheel,
bobbin and spinning spool,
the speed of the needle
as yards of fabric gathered in her lap,
her voice finding, losing, finding again the tune.

"This weather doesn't worry me," she said,
squinting under the bare bulb
that swung beneath the furnace duct,

snow filling up the window well,
house sealed against the cold
that had held us hostage for days,

and the little quiver in her hands
lockstitch after lockstitch,
as her fingers so close to the presser-foot
deftly smoothed and guided the wedding silk.
Never once had she asked me,
"Are you certain? Are you sure?"

"Let It Snow, Let It Snow," she sang,
small squeaky soprano notes
floating up the stairs, me descending.
"How . . ." On the bottom step I hesitated,
adjusting to the half-light,
"How do you do love?"

I see her still. She has quit the machine
and stiffly sits attaching lace
to the hem of a sleeve.
"Oh my," she says, pulling the needle through,
as if she knows what's happened
and what's going to happen to the whole world.

What did I understand of womanhood,
or this woman, for that matter, who survived
South Dakota winters, the Great Depression . . .
me, thinking now, now
she will explain everything?
She knots the thread and bites it off.

WINTER EUCHARIST

Every day begins with the body
thinking about itself,
this toe, this foot, this remarkable knee.

And when the hand travels the thigh, the hip,
the noble sternum,
you consider it might live forever, this body,

that it can remake itself over and over
in a ritual of body
here, under the white cotton bedsheets,

under the quilted comforter,
under the heavy sky,
the space around the body awake now

in the act of remaking,
but even undercover, you can feel the chill
of that inside job mapping the veins,

how their travel to the heart interlaces like a vine
the white bones of a world
you held in your arms all night.

"Not to worry," the bones say,
already working their way back
to where they were hidden.

Dawn collects the cold, deposits it
on the flesh of your lips, your tongue,
weights your lashes, your hair.

Now the weather's turning white again,
eighteen inches by nightfall.
Even predators will fall prey.

You hear the snow move from room to room.
When it stops at your door,
you want it to mean something.

ONLY THE PARTS

Aberdeen, South Dakota, August 1929

My father works in his father's laundry.
All day, steam from the pressing machine,
and his face breaks into a sweat.

He is buttoning a shirt,
slipping the little stay of cardboard
snug under the collar,
placing one sweet-smelling sleeve over the other,

folding the body back to itself.
Square-jawed, tight-bellied,
he prays for a breeze through the open window,
prays for rain.

He once told me there are some things one does
not for money,
not for love,
but simply because one must do them.

Like buttoning a shirt.
Like folding a sleeve.

Sometimes, he said, one is not
the sum of his parts.
He is only the parts.

Perhaps my father understood too much.
When he explained the universe,
his whole frame shook,
and when he slept, he wept.

OF DESIRE

The rabid dog would not let you go,
and there in the doctor's office,
folded into your stomach
because the last shot almost killed you,
you knew you'd have it anyway
to avoid hallucinations,
to avoid foaming at the mouth,
to keep from dying the other way,
so you said, "I'm ready, I'm ready,"
when you knew you were not,

and thought of your father
crossing the playground, waving
his hands in the air to restart his heart,
confessing regrets, those tickets
to heaven or your mother's forgiveness
or yours, which you could not give,
even though the park swelled
with maidenhair, Sweet William,
the indigenous rose,
even though he was kissing your feet.

You'd run your three miles
across the stream, through the culvert
under the freeway,
then back the dusty county road,
past a gathering of strays
stalking through corn rows
some terrified creature, no doubt,
the smell of it
a breath you couldn't breathe,
when the neighbor's black lab,

tongue hanging, abandoned the pack,
scuttled under the barbed wire,
bound toward you as instinct always will,
animal to animal,
bearing burs like medals.
You didn't turn or cry out,
just ran harder
ran farther,
dragging him by the teeth
toward somewhere you called home.

MEDITATION ON A CEILING FAN

Under the whir of the fan
I lie naked and still
and stare at my fingers.

The sheet is white, the air heavy with heat.
I could be vegetable or mineral.
I could be liquid or light.

Shapes drift toward shapelessness,
my hand to not my hand.
I could be an invention of the moon.

The faster they spin, the sooner the blades
abandon their form to motion,
motion to sound the ear knows,

as it knows a field of wheat folding
into wind, the wind
rearranging a sea of crows,

as it knows bare willows at sunset
making thin cuts in the sun.
I'm watching the blades,

imagining the cuts, how they move
from pain to a sound for pain.
It is not so hard to imagine.

What if this hand, five fingers, five nails
with their half-moons,
should fly upward?

What if this hand
falls in love with blades?
What then does the ear know?

TO LIVE IN THAT ROOM

We were taught to love
the pink chintz curtains that filmed
our father's Stanley plums
growing outside the bedroom window
maroon-blue, firm and lush
among their unlobed leaves,

and the second-hand desk painted pink,
the unfinished pine dresser—
three drawers for you, three for me,
sanded smooth—also painted pink,
the wooden knobs etched by our mother—
indeterminate blossoms, two on each knob.

Pink twin headboards with bookshelves,
pink bedframes with drawers,
pink satin quilts littered with plush kittens,

and on the pink shag carpet between beds,
my white hoop skirt
under which hid the misunderstood

private fear that divided us,
and the father you thought loved me more.
I, who knew better, disappeared.

Looking back now, the closet
seems ample, though we fought
for space, for a better way
to live in that room.
You didn't hear me whisper
come away with me. You never knew

across diviner distances
I yearned to talk with you for hours
about that white hoop skirt
tossed on the floor between our beds,
talk for hours about meaning
and the loss of it.

ADDICT

How many times you have practiced
that same passage,
repeated those same first measures,
pounding out Brahms as if
molto passionato meant violent.

How many times you have climbed out
of those same imposing octaves,
discovered how easily you could vanish
breath by breath
and stopped short, terrified

such passion might extinguish the mind,
though it is not the mind,
not the vanishing that disturbs you,
but the dissonant rush and the need
to need it again.

Perhaps you felt a flutter,
a flowering in the lung, and you thought
beauty, thought you could will it,
intended to wait
for as long as it took,

but the violence aroused you—
an epic sounding of the blood.
Perhaps you gazed beyond,
and beyond thought, nothing
but your own hands to save you.

You cannot forgive Brahms,
as if he were responsible, as if beauty
must rage until it ruins everything.
Did Schumann hear it
before he plunged into the Rhine?

You wanted music to be easy,
like opening a window, like
desire without the desire to be touched.
You assumed you could sort out
addiction from the rush,

but it's Brahms who seduced you,
Brahms you accuse,
until you're committed,
attacking the notes with more
than the music can bear.

ARLES AT THREE A.M.

They say it's peaceful,
soft light in the distance,
quiet town at the end of the sky,
orchard in bloom, a shadow
digging its shadow.
They say, See how peaceful.
Look at the little steeple.
They want to hang it in your room.

But the poplars are bare. Can't they see
how bare the poplars are,
gnarled, anonymous?
Do they know the roots moan in the night
while they stand watch awaiting a sign?

You have seen them inspecting the roots.
You see the eye that sees you,
spider cracks on the retina,
and the fog contagious
with blossoms into which you'll plunge,
hold your breath long enough
to be willing to lose.
Breathing could spoil everything.

Outside your room, voices
(perhaps the night nurse and some other)
drag toward morning.
They thicken with kindness.
They say you are awake.

The window arrives first, then branches
tending the wind, then the face
of a body that feeds on air
like the beautiful people

who love from the grave.
They'll bring butterflies to the door,
wings artfully spread,
at least one still alive
with a pin through its thorax,
sunrise startled by the head of the pin.

UNDERWATER

I was playing Brahms when I died,
performing underwater,
the keyboard floating,
my hands disembodied and floating
the way a dream can slowly float

in and out of itself,
and then my mother drifted toward me
her claim of body—
but there was no body,
only the muscles of water.

She was graceful as seaweed,
fish moving through her,
and I thought how lovely their eyes
that depend
on sound or the lack of it.

I wanted to tell her I could feel
the fish move as I moved,
carrying their bodies like messages
among ribs of old ships
winding their way along floating streets

past floating windows, floating doorways,
toward those misty blue flames
that illuminate.
I wanted to tell her dark is the eye
that does not close.

I was playing Brahms, my hands
spanning huge chords
they had never reached before,
and there was my body
stunned with his sudden mind.

TROUBLE WITH MEMORY

Even the moths glow, fumbling at the screen,
and pistachio shells tick after tick
that drop in the bowl between her knees,

while along the hedgerow, magnolias so white
she's sure they will sustain beyond last light
the light.

A luxury of age, she thinks,
when shadows feel like company,
the way they congregate,

soften this lawn of gnats and breathing,
and she would fold such quiet around her . . .
but the crack of a mallet scatters like whispers.

The men are playing croquet again.
Someone laughs.
Someone calls fault.

How long had it been, the last time?
Is it the memory of one, or all of them,
or is it only the body

that finds itself in charcoal,
the underpainting waiting still?
How long had she posed believing

any one of them would do?
Their faces shine, and the wickets shine,
little doorways after the faces go out.

Deep in the bowl, pistachios
shift under, over and around
her fingers fondling the hard-edged shells.

THE BUTTERFLY PROJECT

for the endangered Fender's blue butterfly,
and the Kincaid lupine, its threatened host

When my son bursts through the door
to announce his school project,
dumps all his papers on the floor

to find the list of items necessary to begin—
butterfly net, carbon tet,
insect spreading board,

I accuse the universe,
convinced butterflies endure too much loss,
being too fragile to defend

their right to desire, that terrible kiss
death sometimes remembers
as the predatory flower.

And because once a rare one, blue
like a bruise at the center,
flew into my net, I need to confess.

Though science owned us all that day,
I was the one who volunteered
to pierce the thorax,

impale it on the cork board
while my fourth-grade classmates cheered.
Mr. Kyle praised my steady hand.

I would like to claim the creature's eyes
held me penitent in a death gaze,
but that would be a lie.

Staring at the stilled wings,
that dramatic black border fringed in white,
those 12,000 mini eyes staring back,

I tasted power. Not beauty.
I had not imagined, after it was done,
the mounting pins put away,

how such an act could haunt me,
how late that afternoon,
walking home along the county road,

sudden sunlight on a field of lupine
would explode into butterflies,
the burst of wings collide

not with ghosts,
but ghosts the wings are made of,
and then an ash of iridescence.

I would obsess for days
searching the June sky for some sign
of forgiveness, and even now

as I tuck my son in bed
wings move through me,
phantoms of the pheromonal dark.

SNOW

Say memory touches us just long enough
to reconsider loss,
the way our bodies fold into themselves,

the way last leaves loosen
and ash berries waiting for waxwings
migrating through

cling as if they could cling forever,
fermenting because it is theirs to do.

When the snow begins, it does not fall,
but encloses, like fog,
perspires along the streets, the gutters,

wrinkles window ledges,
pushes whispers under the door.
Yes. Yes, we whisper.

Say snow renews a way
to love by will—

snow above us, snow below us,
we sweep our arms back and forth,
making angels in the snow

as if memory of feeling were feeling,
wings without the body freezing
silenced by the cold.

Am I the only one who thinks
nothing can hurt us now?

UNDER ICE

. . . nothing save a little thread, descanted on by art and industry.
—Thomas Fuller

These are the wings of the lacemaker,
these are the lacemaker's children,
these are the spreading intimacies of frost

frivolous as pantylace or eyelets
of leaves filleted at the vein.
Winter's come, no doubt about that.

We'll sleep in this hum of stitches
freezing to glass, and wake
with pupil unstitched to see through,

filigree of cold that splays
into breaking light, the light,
gossamer cracks growing like ivy.

This is *punto a fogliami*, this nuptial veil
or shroud, this is point
and counterpoint revisited

until the lace bug—having attached
to the midrib of sycamore leaves
her tiny tumors of egg, having taught them

to suck midsummer to frost—ceases all her art,
unhooking silver from interior silver,
wing from disintegrating wing.

THIS COULD BE THE DAY

Before dawn, before the neighbor's lights go on,
before tomcats trek across the yard
and the yew begins its morning shiver
to disrobe that first weight of snow,

before the garbage truck rumbles and grunts,
before night sprinklers in the park
sputter and pull back into their winter holes,
before a bitter wind drifts down from the hills

to paralyze vagrant warblers who thought
not yet, not yet, and have lingered too long,
she is slipping into her long silk underwear,
pulling on wool socks, turtleneck,

sweatpants, hooded fleece jacket.
She listens for water in the teapot to boil.
She likes the growing comfort of her body
inside all these layers, the awareness

of her hands, still unmittened, how they
wrap around the warm cup of tea.
She's fascinated by the bend of her wrist,
the flexible blue veins, strangely compliant,

that can appear and disappear so easily,
the opposable thumb which even now
as she tips the cup, finds a way to serve.
She likes the sudden consciousness

of dawn wandering through the fog
that's wandering too, dimming porch lamps,
window sills, the insistent chill
fingering under the door.

She had fondled the sounds—
registers crackling and grumbling,
rungs of the rocking chair wearing away,
mirror over the mantle reflecting

the way a new day crawled onto the stove,
polished cookware hanging from a low beam,
dishrag draped over the faucet.
everything as it was, and should be.

Why this morning is it the untracked snow
and that great horned owl all night still calling?
Why today does she envy the art of cold
against the window, how the glass bears witness

to first sunlight shuddering
across ferns of hoarfrost, ferns of ferns
growing small and smaller
copies of themselves, one could say with love?

And yet she pauses before the word,
a melancholy. It's patterns she thinks of now.
The still occupied bed is a measure.
The upside-down nuthatch at the same feeder,

and how snow must surely hear inside itself
the snow, how everything that's begun
must begin again. This could be the day.
How long would it take to forget,

not on purpose of course, but with abandon,
the troubling intimacy of a pulse,
a breath, a body so close she had lost her own,
one could say, with love? One could say it.

IV

CHOPIN IN THE RAIN

All night it rained
and the rain did not hurry.
I woke to the drone of it
steady on the roof,
an incessant stir in the leaves.

My fingertip pulsed,
the little finger of the left hand,
the one that had practiced hour after hour
to drop with the exact same weight
on the same A flat,

practiced to repeat and repeat
the same tone
without spasm, without lurches,
practiced to fall
like small, matched pearls

heavy as mercury, liquid as rain
deepening its quiet in the rain bed,
thickening the stream.
Sostenuto, the prelude says.
What it means: endure.

Pianissimo, it says.
What it means: soft as frost
at the edge of feathers falling,
deep as roots disappear
without disappearing.

Chopin must have understood
it's the soft that's hard,
must have known
how the wrist can seize up,
the hand freeze,

the finger ache from repetition
in its effort to withhold.
He let the thumb take over,
repeat and repeat
until he could not resist

that ominous drumming in the head,
the need to grow louder
a kind of violence—and the rain
growing louder to appease the need.
He understood the rain,

how it soothes the saplings
or bends them to the ground,
how it seeps into everything—
joints, muscle, sinew,
the heart, especially the heart—

how it can score the stone.
It's the soft that's hard,
that must sink
first to the key's resistance,
then deeper still for sound.

This morning, the window fills with rain.
The keys feel slippery and cool,
my hands too stiff, fingers too anxious.
I close the Steinway
and with a soft cloth

polish and polish the mahogany lid.
I do not hurry.
The grain turns to current,
current to river,
the river to dank tropic aromas

of rain forests, swirls of bird, ticking
insects that thrive in the underquiet
where the mahogany grew.
I polish until rain
can see itself in the wood.

GRAVITY

. . . try as we may to make a silence, we cannot.
—John Cage

If she props the lid open,
draws her finger across the harp,

leaves a trail through
films of air settled there,

and breathes as though the sounding board
can rescue breath,

surely someone will hear it,
the pedal sustain it so much like a prayer

she should be kneeling.
But she is not kneeling.

Anchored from the hip, stiff-backed,
head tipped forward,

she turns one page, then another,
lips parted, hum of (could it be light?)

purling through her veins.
What has ever felt so heavy

as her hands floating above the ivory.
without touching, never touching

that translucent whisper of keys below
and hardly space enough between?

Is it for silence, or gravity,
her arms ache with music?

RELEARNING THE APPASSIONATA

He is of himself alone, and it is to this aloneness
that all music owes its being.
> Egyptian inscription quoted in Schiller's
> "The Mission of Moses"

i.

Beethoven must have suspected
before the hum and buzz,
before the hot terror seized him.

How long could he ignore
the moon rattling inside his head
without an avalanche of bells and starfish,
how long contain the rage?
"Whore!" he must have shouted.

And yet, pianissimo he wrote,
note after note, deliberate as grief
until grief released his hands.

ii.

His hands flee from the keys and shake
like two strange mutes, his skin an overload
of moonlight,

his genitals on fire, his body
terrified by this wild thing that dances in him,
every silence bolder than before.

Do not tell the deaf how many ears God has
or the kind of music played in heaven.
Make, he says, whatever love is left.

iii.

After the applause, after the hall empties,
after the houselights dim and go out,
and the last door sucks shut,
still he turns the pages of his score.

iv.

It's a matter of timing.
To remain passive and still.
To send my heart back to its stone.
And yet always there is Beethoven,
always his deafness coming on,
and he is mad to hear whatever will
and will not yield.

I go down in the body.
I come up for breath.
Should I confess the bones too bright,
nerves too violent, undercurrents of the blood
too deep, too loud?
Should I confess the little deaths,
resolutions unresolved,
all those interior mouths kissing the dark?

The heart, too, is remarkable
seized by silence loosening itself
the way waves loosen what they too much love.

I am learning the *Appassionata* again.
Tonight, he says, let the body be sound.

AT SUNSET

Just ten miles from home, somewhere
between Tekoa and a sharp turn west,
late afternoon sun collides with the silo,
erupts in pieces, a fallout of sunlight
that ignites the air,

and I am holding the road in my hands,
feeling it swerve one direction,
then the other,
little worlds at every curve
spinning out of control.

Already there are the dead
and half-dead along the ragged shoulder
and the stranded squeal of tires
left at the scene,
contortions of metal still at war.

I was headed home, but already
I'd forgotten the way.
Sparks glance off the hood,
little fires at work in the ditches,
wipers too burdened with ash,

shrapnel and glass,
a confusion of fumes and flames
and still the universe hurrying
toward some other emergency
not yet defined.

On this backroad let's suppose
I'm the only witness,
and someone says, you go on home now,
you hear, you go on home.

And let's suppose
I don't know what that means.
Will home define itself?
Does it emerge reinvented
each time I survive?
Or does it hide in the fierce eye of the sun?

TIME SIGNATURES

It's never an ordinary day.
If nudged awake, the dead would tell you so.
                              —Gary Soto

Because of daffodils, we know
that winter can surprise us
with enough warm days to trust
in promises, that fields will reveal
lush swaths of gold, roads reappear
and squirrels uncover
secret stashes from beneath the snow.

Because of primroses, we know
April can save us from the cold,
even though the almanac
warns a bitter wind might freeze
the lake again just thick enough
for us to trust the ice once more,
drop the line, and not be missed 'til dusk.

Because of milkweed, gray pods
stiff along the drainage ditch,
silver parachutes entangling in the sumacs'
late blood-summer red,
we surmise our monarchs will return
with memory, or memory spent,
that blush of extraordinary light.

Today, sunset at 6:28.
Still, feathergrass in the air,
still one pale peach rose, one
blue-tinged nuthatch we've never seen before
foraging the gutter, mostly upside down,
chickadees ticking on the roof,
time we had not planned but waited for.

Perhaps you take my hand.
Perhaps I take yours.
Will we wait until the cold begins,
not a mere shiver, but cold
that creeps into our feet, crawls
by marrow into a sound we recognize—
that familiar—still beating?

Because asters wait to bloom
so deeply violet in September,
moonlight buzzes into spaces
bees abandoned for the night,
long into October
neon petals, honeyed for the frost,
shining, shining.

SHELTERED IN PLACE

You called them song dogs,
painted them on road signs,
carved them on church doors,
twisted them from junkyard metal
with elongated necks and engorged throats.

You said the moon emerged
from their first howl
and turned their howls to music.
I listened hard for it.
That was years ago.

Last night we thought we heard them
out beyond Margret Eddie's place
where lawns turn to prairie,
and the last crossroad takes off east
toward the foothills,

our bedroom window open to viburnum,
crabapples, omens
of a cold front bringing the storm
that would seal us in.
Then the wind all night,

all day, all night again, shaking branches
free of blossoms,
thousands of pink and white petals,
choked gutters, confettied
roads, patios, window sills,

our bed quilt heavy with petals.
And still they fall, even after.
We are familiar lovers lying together.
Passion and words
fold and unfold us gentler now.

Sometimes you say I sing in my sleep.
Sometimes we pray to something unseen
to save us from something unseen.
But always the coyotes.
From the quarantined quiet, we listen.

IN SPITE OF QUARANTINE

Remember how first came silence,
then branches heavy with song.
Someone said, Listen.
Someone asked,
Have they been here all along?

In spite of quarantine, the sky
turned to wings,
winter to spring, yards to gardens.
Remember how first came loneliness,
then, almost overnight, solitude?

We walked the streets we'd only driven—
step by step, by breath, by name—
Elk Ridge, Crestview, Palouse River Drive,
Daphne here, five-foot yucca there,
hedgerows of chickadees.

We heard our feet crunch
down alleys we'd never noticed,
hollyhocks in the wind,
two small boys in the gravel building roads
with a yellow jeep and a hoe.

Late autumn, scattering bone meal
where the tulips had bloomed,
working the white powder into tired beds,
watching it blend and disappear,
I did not think of the bulbs or the bone,

but the scent of dropped plums,
the latticed shade of bared branches
and the work, always the work,
how it goes on,
the sound of steel tines raking the loam.

A curious sweet weariness
quiets itself, and me
imagining what if there were no dreams
but only this sound as long as winter
scoring the caverns of sleep.

REPLANTING THE IRIS

If they're not in the next world, I don't want to be there.
—W.S. Merwin

Deep in the soil, my hands unearth
the crowded clumps of iris,
nodes and internodes,
buds and old rhizomes locked together,
too long fiercely entangled
and competing roots.

It is my job to break them apart,
clip their roots, remove
the mushy, the smelly,
the borer infested,
re-bury the healthy, but not too deep.
Even in winter, they need to feel the light.

Already I've scissored the leaves,
brushed the dirt,
the occasional crawling thing,
from each carbuncled corm.
Already I've raked and sifted the soil,
readied the bed.

Who will make this book of the sick,
book of survivors, book of the dead?
Who will post the charts,
the nightmares
my fingers have almost loved,
almost understood?

WINTER HERON

Even now, in the long slow
whitening of trees
and air and everything that breathes,

lungs weighted, limbs weighted,
the ache settled,
bulge and spread of roots stunned,

even now as I wonder
at my unruly praise
for wild stars roosting in the birch

and this blue-feathered cold,
I remember how uneasy
the quiet on the Lochsa last summer

when a heron, severed from its shadow
by haunted water,
severed from the water

by its pretense of sleep,
the stationary eye not an eye exactly,
but the brain of an eye

blue as beauty in its cold heart,
possessed all the waters of heron.
No purer spirit poised.

LIKE AN ESMERALDAS WOODSTAR

I would like to go dancing.
I'd wear green pearls and crinoline,
flutter my heart twenty beats a second,
sip from trumpets,
summon the hinterlands,
electrify.

I would like to go dancing,
circle and glide as a satellite
without touching all orbit long
the curve of its moon.

Not in grand crystal ballrooms
but on rooftops
I'd like to go dancing,
sassy strut, moonwalk,
waggle like bees,
wear red leather boots
and a headpiece of ribbons and plumes.

I'd dance barefoot
when the sky turns all brooding
and swans lift off
trailing their noises like song.
I would arch my back, stretch my neck,
inhale till my lungs carried me
across rivers, set me down
in lands delirious with dancing.

Not heavy-headed poppies
red-silked, one-eyed,
nor waves of new wheat
have loved dancing so much.

As mirrors dance
their own separate waltzes
secretly, when I pass them in the dark,
I would dance.
I'd promenade, weave—
one-two-three, one-two-three—
shimmer, and bow.

And where the colt bounded freely
through belly-high grass,
where now the mare shivers, already snow
spotting her withers, frosting her mane,
she is shaking, shaking it off
with the nostrils of her,
the shoulders of her.

For the history of her through the universe
even as quiet fills up the cold
I will dance.

BODY BE FLUTE

i.

They dine in wakes, scatter
with grunts and hisses

the carcasses they feed on.
They mate for life.

The vagrants arrived from before,
or so it is written,

with a nine-foot wingspan
and hunger for the dead.

Can we who try to explain ourselves
in the house of this flesh

help but wonder why
from the bone of this bird came music?

ii.

Did she scratch it out of the earth
or find it in the grip of angels?

Did she hold it to the light, imagine
stars crawling in and out,

or press to her ear hums and kisses,
labyrinths of elbows and knees,

hips and hallucinations,
stamp her bare feet, put on feathers,

feel the exhilaration of uplift,
the weight of down.

How long did she stroke it, admire it,
oil it with the oil of her hands,

this bone of the bird of buff body
and broad wings, of white neck ruff

and hooked beak,
of the survival-resting heart?

How long before she thought
to put it to her lips and blow?

iii.

It seems obvious now—a hollow bone.
Any child would have done it.

But when did she think to pierce the hole,
and after the first, did she think

the second, the third, and so on
until there were five?

Who, before Pythagoras, walked the universe
searching for mysteries?

Who, before Kepler,
graphed the orbit of heavenly bodies,

found the origin of harmonic order
in the alignment of their songs?

How many, before Grieg, heard
floating about in morning ethers

the pentatonic scale?
As perhaps did she, who made

of this bone this instrument,
brought it to her lips,

placed her fingers on the five holes,
closed her eyes and played.

Of time that sleeps in echoes,
what shape does it take

when it comes into our hands,
when it flees with our breath from this bone?

ACKNOWLEDGEMENTS

My deepest gratitude to my writing mentors, Robert Wrigley, Ron McFarland, and Heather McHugh, without whom this book would have never come to fruition. A special thanks to Paul Lindholdt for his ongoing encouragement and insights, and to so many other writers and friends along this journey, including my pals in Fort Russell Writers, who also generously read these poems and offered input for which I am truly grateful.

My gratitude to the editors of the following publications in which some of these poems first appeared in their original form:

Antigonish Review, "This Could Be the Day"

Cadence of Hooves: A Celebration of Horses, "Between a Man and a Woman"

Calyx, "At Sunset"

Chariton Review, "Before the Snow," "This Is Not a Poem About Birds," "The Photo I Kept," "Trouble with Memory"

Chautauqua, "Milkman"

Cirque, "Absence," "Trouble with Minnows," "Sheltered in Place"

Concho, "Nightwalk"

Ecology of Desire, "Our Daily Bread"

Flint Hills Review, "Chopin in the Rain"

Hubbub, "Trouble with Holy Places"

Lost Coast Review, "Sunday Drive"

Malahat Review, "Night Fishing"

Midwest Review, "South Dakota Saturday Night,"
"In the Dry Season"

Poems and Plays, "Vow," "Stroke," "Bear on the Road to the
Sun," "Of Desire," "Addict"

Rhino, "Underwater"

South Carolina Review, "To Live in That Room"

Talking River Review, "My Mother's Dance," "Hometown
Burial," "Roadkill," "Snow," "The Butterfly Project"

Tar River Poetry, "Winter Heron"

The Cape Rock, "The Visit"

The Turnip Trucks, "Relearning the Appassionata"

The Threepenny Review, "The Last Theorem," "Daguerreotype
of Unidentified Woman"

Touchstone, "Blessing"

Trestle Creek Review, "What My Grandmother Said," "In Spite
of Quarantine"

Weber Studies, "Under Ice"

Willow Spring, "Whispers," "Meditation on a Ceiling Fan"

Xavier Review, "Manatee," "Gravity."

About the Author

Georgia Tiffany, a Spokane, Washington native, holds graduate degrees from Indiana University and the University of Idaho. Since high school she has taught piano and has performed with orchestras and in faculty recitals. At Mead High in Spokane, where she taught for almost twenty years, her students won numerous creative writing awards in regional and national competitions. Her poems have appeared in scores of literary magazines including *Antigonish*, *Midwest Review*, *South Carolina Review*, *Threepenny Review*, *Weber*, and *Willow Springs*. Her work appears in the *Poets of the American West* anthology. Night Owl Press published her limited-edition chapbook, *Cut from the Score*, in 2006. Georgia has given readings and conducted workshops in states from Washington and Idaho to Ohio and Tennessee. The late Mike Shields, longtime editor of *Orbis*, wrote, "Georgia Tiffany's poetry . . . shimmers with marvelously inventive images and phrases, magic and mystery, at the same time bringing a concern for other human beings: every poem is in some way a dialogue with the reader. I consider her work of major literary importance." *Body Be Sound* was a semifinalist for the 2023 Lexi Rudnitsky First Book Prize in Poetry.

Printed in the USA
CPSIA information can be obtained
at www.ICGtesting.com
JSHW022121141123
51943JS00001B/1